The Birth of a
New Tradition

Story by Ramsey Asmar   Illustrations by Lane Yerkes

RSVP
**RAINTREE
STECK-VAUGHN**
P U B L I S H E R S
The Steck-Vaughn Company

Austin, Texas

To my parents for their love and encouragement.
To all the people who cherish their freedom. — **R.A.**

To my children, Christopher and Jonathan. — **L.Y.**

Library of Congress Cataloging-in-Publication Data

Asmar, Ramsey, 1980–
   The birth of a new tradition / story by Ramsey Asmar; illustrations by Lane Yerkes.
   p.   cm. — (Publish-a-book)
   Summary: A young Russian gymnast reflects upon the changes in his life and gymnastic career as the Soviet Union dissolves into separate countries.
   1. Soviet Union — History — 20th century — Juvenile fiction.
2. Children's writings. [1. Soviet Union — History — 20th century — Fiction.   2. Gymnasts — Fiction.   3. Children's writings.]   I. Yerkes, Lane, ill.   II. Title.   III. Series.
PZ7.A8377Bi   1993   [Fic] — dc20   92–35284
                                                                                                    CIP
ISBN 0–8114–3583–0   AC

Sergei stood on the platform, arms outstretched, bracing himself for his final flip. His heart beat loudly in his chest. He glanced at the crowd that was waiting quietly for his finale. Thoughts flooded his mind. How long he had prepared for this competition! How much he wanted and deserved to win!

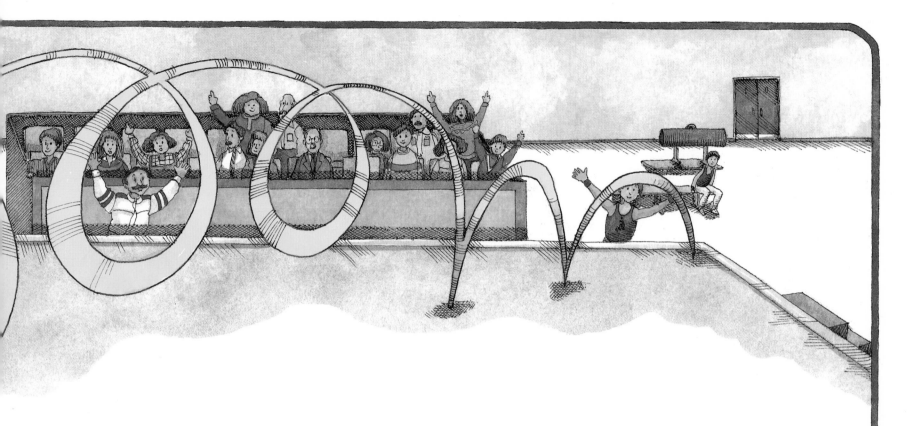

The sweat made his shirt cling to his muscular body. He pushed back his straight black hair and took a deep breath. Suddenly, he ran across the platform, somersaulted a few times, triple-flipped in the air, and landed solidly on his feet. The crowd roared with excitement. He had done it! After five long years of training, he had finally won the right to perform in the gymnastics parade on Revolution Day.

Sergei swelled with pride. He was now the best gymnast in his town. His parents rushed out and embraced him. His best friend, Vladi, who had won the championship the year before, congratulated him. Now Sergei knew that he would be going to Moscow to perform with the country's best gymnasts.

During the next few weeks, all Sergei did was practice. Hours and hours every day, he worked on perfecting his routine. His confidence was at its highest point. Vladi would join him sometimes, and his accounts of the parade made Sergei even more excited and impatient for the event.

The mood in his country did not match Sergei's, however. The political, economic, and social situation was deteriorating. Jobs and food were scarce. Sergei's parents were luckier than most, since they had steady jobs. The Soviet people were very unhappy. They envied the Western lifestyle. Some of the Soviet countries were already demanding their independence.

13

While Sergei was busy preparing for the Revolution Day Parade that would celebrate Communism, his country was falling apart. In the back of his mind, he was aware of the turmoil around him. Then, it happened. The people took down Lenin's statue, and the Soviet Union was no more.

In school, Sergei and his friends had been taught
that the American way was wrong. But deep down in
his heart, Sergei always wished he lived in America and
had the freedom that Americans had. He wished he had
all the wonderful toys that American children played
with. This made him feel guilty, as if he was betraying
his country. Now, the Soviet Union was trying to
become like America!

Things started to change too fast for Sergei. Now that there was no more Communism, he knew that there would be no Revolution Day Parade. That tradition had ended. On the day his coach gently broke the news to him, he rushed out of the gym, slamming the door behind him. He started running and did not stop until his lungs hurt with every intake of breath. He didn't care about anything. All he could think of was missing his chance to make his dream come true.

Sergei sat and leaned against the wall of an old building. He closed his eyes and let his memories take him back to earlier parades. He was only five years old the first time he had been there. Sitting on his father's shoulders, gripping his curly hair for dear life, his eyes were wide with fascination at the sight of the amazing gymnasts, musicians, and marching bands.

The crowd around him was pushing to get a better view. He could almost hear their cheers now. He had strained his neck to keep the gymnasts in sight as long as possible, but the parade had ended too soon for him.

The Revolution Day trip to Moscow had become a yearly tradition for his family. It was his favorite time of the whole year. He spent it with his parents, eating delicious borscht and katah bread in restaurants, listening to the music, and watching the parade. What inspired Sergei most were the gymnasts. He wanted to be just as good as they were and perform in the parade with them.

Only the best gymnasts in the country were chosen, and he knew he could be the best. He and Vladi had practiced together, pushing each other on. Watching Vladi perform last year was his final push. Now, it was supposed to be his turn.

But, there was no parade. Sergei was excited and
sad at the same time. He wanted the changes in his
country, for everything has to change. There was
a lot of work ahead, and it was up to his generation
to make Russia a great country once more. He would
miss the parade, though. Why did that have to end?
Couldn't they keep it? They could celebrate their
new-found freedom. Yes! Freedom Day Parade!

Sergei ran all the way back to the gym. He had a great idea about how to save the parade and couldn't wait to tell his coach.

Ramsey Asmar, the twelve-year-old author of **The Birth of a New Tradition**, wrote the story in the sixth grade at Boulan Park Middle School in Troy, Michigan. This is where he currently lives with his parents, Leda and Basim, and his eight-year-old brother, Michael. His father is a pediatrician, and his mother is a registered nurse. Ramsey was sponsored in the Publish-a-Book Contest by Alicia Hutton, his language arts teacher.

Ramsey started by doing research on traditions and customs in different countries. Then, influenced by the events in the Soviet Union and the media coverage of the Winter and Summer Olympics, he picked the Revolution Day Parade and a fictional champion gymnast for his story.

Ramsey is a straight A student. His best subjects are science and math. He loves school and greatly enjoys the challenge of academic competitions. Music is an important part of Ramsey's life. He plays the violin in his school orchestra and has been an outstanding piano student for four years.

In his spare time, Ramsey likes to read. His favorite authors are Madeleine L'Engle and J. R. R. Tolkien. He collects stamps and baseball and basketball cards. He also enjoys playing computer games. Ramsey likes to swim and play basketball and tennis, but he enjoys watching all sports. His favorite pastime is attending a Detroit Lions game.

Ramsey discovered that he enjoyed writing stories in the fourth grade. The next year he won the Michigan Future Problem Solving Scenario writing competition. This year, in addition to winning the 1992 Raintree/Steck-Vaughn Publish-a-Book Contest, Ramsey was chosen as the first recipient of the Alexander Fischbein Young Writer's Award. It was established in memory of Alex Fischbein, a writer who died at the age of ten, to encourage young students to write and submit their works for publication.

Ramsey is not sure what he will do in the future. He is interested in medicine and law. Whatever he does, he will continue to enjoy writing.

The twenty honorable-mention winners in the **1992 Raintree/Steck-Vaughn Publish-a-Book Contest** were Heidi Roberts of Dresden, Maine; Jessica McCulla of Mesa, Arizona; Kristine Laughlin of Mount Laurel, New Jersey; Tori Miner of Franklin, Connecticut; Brittany Kok of Decatur, Illinois; Hilary Manske of Clintonville, Wisconsin; Mandy Baldwin of Bothell, Washington; Kristin Yoshimoto of Honolulu, Hawaii; Arwen Miller of Kent, Ohio; Jessica Martin of Wauwatosa, Wisconsin; Jessa Queyrouze of Mandeville, Louisiana; Kay-Lynn Walters of Fostoria, Ohio; Karen Lauffer of Edgewater, Maryland; Karey Vaughn of Somerset, Pennsylvania; Matthew Kuzio of Mandeville, Louisiana; Leonard Ford of Germantown, Tennessee; Carolyn Hack of Overland Park, Kansas; Emily Levasseur of Hudson, New Hampshire; Christina Miller of Port Jefferson, New York; and Shawna Smith of Hays, Kansas.

Lane Yerkes graduated from the Philadelphia College of Art in 1972 and began his career as a freelance illustrator. His assignments have covered editorial, newspaper, advertising, book publishing, fabric design, and magazine illustration. Lane is married with two sons and has just recently moved to the southwest coast of Florida, where he now has his studio.